Held Hostage
by a Stranger

Held Hostage by a Stranger

A Message from the MOST HIGH

Fatimah Mahassan Jackson

Library of Congress Control Number:		2013919621
ISBN:	Hardcover	978-1-4931-2307-0
	Softcover	978-1-4931-2306-3
	eBook	978-1-4931-2308-7

This book was printed in the United States of America.

Rev. date: 12/26/2013

To order additional copies of this book, contact:
Xlibris LLC
1-888-795-4274
www.Xlibris.com
Orders@Xlibris.com
142979

DEDICATION

The **LORD** is my Shepherd!

Thank you **Mommy** "Sheila" (may her soul rest peacefully-6/17/13) for putting my jumbled words into understandable sentences. She encouraged me beyond compare, to take my time and keep on writing. As the words were pouring out, she kept me calm, level headed and at peace through it all. Not one negative word came out of her mouth about what I was going through while I was writing. Mommy, I know you are looking down on me. I love you.

My **Husband** "Taheem" my Love, I tried to keep you free and clear from my numerous feelings while writing. I know some of them spilled out and over lapped. Thank you for being there. I love you more today than yesterday.

AUTHOR'S NOTE

HE came to me in a dream, so much so fast. HE told me of my ups and downs, HE told me of my past. He said "Your sins are forgiven". HE said "Salvation is free, so cast your cares, cast your cares on me".

Before you read this book, this book about my life; ask GOD for understanding, clarity and the release of all your strife. Most of all, pray for the awakening of your Spirit, for the LORD is calling.

INTRODUCTION

The world is full of encounters/messengers and messages sent by divine intervention. You will never know when they will come, but they are always at the right time. Expectation is one of my many issues. You see I expect a message in all things and from all people.

Messages help guide us through life. They help us to keep our heads on straight. They bring us back to reality and they remind us that GOD is always near. If you listen closely, you can hear GOD speak to you through the wind, the trees, the sunshine and the rain. Encounters are very, very special meetings. There is an unexplainable, wonderful presence. It's like the whole world stops rotating on its axis. It's really bright and there is no sound, it's very peaceful.

You know we always try to run form our fate and that makes our journey that much harder which prolongs the inevitable. I do not have the words to express the thankfulness I have for receiving these messages and telling people about them and what a profound effect they have had on my life. None of us are worthy of such a wonderful gift, especially not me. Someone in the women's circle group told me "GOD does not expect us to be perfect just faithful". That particular message was meant just for me at that exact time. I broke out crying the very moment because I was beating myself up about something from my past and my present. I will not always question any aspect of the messages/encounters. I am just thankful to receive them.

With all my heart and soul from the Spirit of the LORD, I believe in GOD's power. The place GOD takes us requires a lot of faith, patience, prayer and focus. Always ask for GOD's will and get ready for **your** message.

I noticed the stranger when he walked into the room and sat in the back by the door on the other side. He wore a bright orange and yellow jogging suit and carried three medium size bags. I don't know if he is homeless or if he just wondered in off the street. I watched him for a while because he seemed peculiar to me. As I watched he was saying hello to various people. Well, it was time for a break and I walked pass the stranger. I heard him prophesying to someone at that time and I thought to myself "Oh, I wonder if he will have a message for me"? I stared even harder at the stranger as I walked by but he didn't even look at me. So I turned my head and went on my way. At lunch later that day, a group of acappella singers performed and the Holy Spirit came upon me during one of their songs. The song is called "No Ways Tired". That was my first message of the day. It was confirmation that GOD knew my struggles. As the song went on my heart was pricked many, many times and at one point I stood to my feet praising and thanking GOD for the song the message and the singers. What a blessing.

At the end of the song I went up to the group and thanked them for blessing me. I didn't have the words to express how I truly felt but they got the picture, for my eyes were filled with joy. I made my way back to the conference room to get ready for the second half and it went by pretty fast. At the end of the day everyone was headed out of the room and we all went to the lobby to greet the vendors and talk about the day's events. I noticed the stranger was still sitting in the back of the room and I walked in his direction in silent anticipation. I tried to keep my cool so I would not draw any attention to myself. When I got close to the stranger he looked at me and said "what"? At that moment I was speechless and said nothing, but for some reason I could not turn away. In the back of my mind I knew the reason; I believed he had a message from the LORD just for me and I wanted my message. I needed my message. I stood there in silence and the stranger was silent and said nothing else to me. I began to think "was I wrong" and started to walk away. Then I turned and looked back one last time hoping he would say something else to me. I held my breath and hoped in my heart the LORD would speak and then the stranger said "ok, you passed the test I was seeking". I exhaled with joy and relief. I looked at the stranger and smiled. I don't remember what I said but I know I smiled with much joy.

The stranger looked at me and said "I don't have to prophesy to you because you have it in you". Still staring at him I kept very quiet. He spoke again saying "you're like the woman with the issue of blood hoping to just, trying to just touch maybe HE will". I just stared as my eyes watered because he was right. I wanted my message; I needed my message from the LORD. I felt like my life was in turmoil and I needed guidance. Then the stranger said, "Come, walk with me". So we headed to the lobby where all the people and vendors were chatting.

We sat down the stranger sighed and began to tell me things about my life; past, present and future. There was so much hope in my heart and mind as I listened to every word.

He said, "You are a special girl and you look famous, you are beautiful and unique and GOD is with you and still working on you". He said "I am here to take your hurt'. Then the stranger asked, "Do you want to talk"? I really did not know what to say so I just stared at him with my watery eyes. Again he said "I am here to take your hurt, you cry because you are sad and hurt. Hurt from all the things that have happened to you and through it all you stayed close to GOD". He said, "You have done some bad things but you are a good person. All your life you have been a good person. You know about Job? Job lost everything but remained close to GOD and faithful to GOD". He continued and said "You are not broken it is a test, it is a test. You were given to your husband your husband was not given to you. Your husband is broken not you. You need to be loved in a special way and you did not come here for yourself".

As the stranger was talking I was listening and crying at the same time. I really cared about what he was saying. He paused and then continued. "Wow, you are like the woman with the issue of blood and you have trusted me to talk to you for a long time, you keep reaching and hoping". That is how I felt because there was so much going on in my life the past three years. It's been devastating for me and I felt like I couldn't take any more. From the moment I saw him in the room I knew he was out of place. You have to be mindful of strangers in those situations. You never know who will deliver your message.

The stranger then asked me a couple of questions about Abraham. One of the answers I gave was wrong. The stranger said "Abraham was faithful to GOD and you are also faithful to GOD. GOD loves you and is always with you. We have been talking for a long time. I see in your eyes that you trust me, you trust this encounter". Then he asked, "Are you being held against your will? Are you being held hostage by a stranger? You don't know me but you see in me what I am gifted with". Then he said "By the way, that is the name of your book; Held hostage by a Stranger". Then he laughed. The stranger went on to say "You are spoiled; people have given to you all your life haven't they? Again I tell you, your husband is stubborn, your eyes are beautiful and unique and your hair and everything about you is special. You look famous".

The stranger said "Remember Job? His wife wanted him to choose her side and curse GOD for what happened in their lives, but Job refused and stayed faithful to GOD". "You are barren because marriage is a sacred event". Let me ask you: "If you had to choose between your mother and your husband, who would you choose and why"? I was shocked at the question. At first I just stared because I was afraid to answer. Then the stranger said "You did not come here for yourself, you came here as an intercessor for your mother and your husband". I immediately broke down crying because he knew the truth. I told him that my mother had been sick and I was afraid of losing her. He said "why"? I said "Because I need her". After a few seconds of silence, which seemed like an eternity, the stranger said "Your mother was spared because she is a praying woman, she prays for you". I said, "Yes, she does". He said "She is fine it is your husband who is broken. He shook his head and repeated "You are spoiled, your husband is broken and you seek GOD. You have to face the truth, when you leave here you will be different." The stranger tilted his head and said "You know you have helped me in this process". "If you need me you can find me". I told the stranger I will find him and that I have to go. He said "Let's pray". He prayed for my wisdom, knowledge, comfort, courage and peace. He ended the prayer saying "LORD she will look for you, buy she has already found you". We then parted ways.

In my heart it was a bitter sweet message. On one hand, I was truly thankful for the LORD speaking to me through the stranger helping me through life. On the other hand, it was upsetting to hear what I have always known. I have to remember to never doubt and know that GOD is everywhere and always with me.

The thought of me writing a book stuck in my head for only a moment while the stranger was talking. Later on that day I thought to myself, "me, write a book? I don't write stories". I know I limit myself and in the process I probably block many blessings. Stupid me, I should just go with it. You know when GOD tells us to do something we always seem to hesitate and try to ignore the message. Instead, we should say "Thank you LORD" get it done and move on with our lives.

At times I feel that I am not worthy of GOD's love because of the things I have done in my life. Although we are forgiven of our past sins if we confess them to GOD. We must also believe in our heart. I love GOD so much and I pray that I never lose that love. I don't know about you, but I need GOD's love to survive.

As I dwell on the path of my unforeseen future, I know I am not worthy of the encounters with these messengers. I will never be pure enough (as pure as I want to be anyway) but I thank the LORD that messages come my way.

After trying to get pregnant for 11 years using every modern technology available, I finally conceived in 2008. We were so happy and excited. I told some of my friends and one of them said "Don't get too attached". I didn't think about what they said at that moment because I was on cloud nine about my miracle. Especially since I am not barren anymore a label I had given myself years ago. Yes, I labeled myself as barren for so many years. I was really stressed but I wanted to give my husband a family. Earlier that year we talked and decided to give it one more chance. This time I gave 300% and was overly focused on family. We went back to our doctor and she sent us to another fertility specialist. I was examined and tested to no end and the doctor came to the conclusion that I did not need any medications to help me conceive. All the results were normal, normal can you believe it? The doctor was puzzled and very optimistic. She sent us home and told us to try the old fashioned way. The doctor told us to pick up an ovulation kit and to come in for weekly blood tests. I was frustrated and thought it was a waste of time because well, been there done that and don't want to go back. I went to the doctor several times to get the blood tests so the doctor would know the right time for me to conceive. Then one day the doctor called and said "Ok, it's time to try" and so we did. I was nervous and excited at the same time. My husband was very positive and yet balanced with his emotions, as usual.

That next month my cycle was late. My birthday was two days away and my cycle was 4 weeks late. I had recently started a new job so I was not focused on my cycle being early or late. My cycle had been late before the only difference was I smelled Bar-B-Q and wanted Celery. I didn't eat or drink much those days and my coworkers had been teasing me about being pregnant and after weeks and days of teasing I became curious and wanted to know. I stopped by the drug store on the way home from work and my heart was racing. I wondered if it could be true. When I got home my husband wasn't there yet so I paced the floor until I got the courage to take the test. It was positive! I was shocked. Was I pregnant? Is it true, is it real? It's a miracle! It's a miracle! I was supposed to be barren, childless, not any more Thank you LORD!

A few days later, we got off work early so I went to my primary doctor's office to change an appointment date. It was very hot that August and I was tired and stressed for some reason. When I finally arrived at the doctor's office the receptionist said "You look strange, are you alright"? I said "Well, I do feel a little funny". She said "sit down we are going to get the doctor to take a look at you right away". I said I am fine I came only to change my appointment date. I just need some water, I am thirsty". The receptionist said "You look dehydrated come with me". She took me to the back and immediately had a nurse come to my aid. I felt exhausted and miserable, I just wanted to go home and lay down in my bed. It was very hard for the nurse to draw blood because I was so severely dehydrated. After she took blood I had to give a urine sample and it was official, I was pregnant.

The doctor examined me and said that I need to go the OBGYN as soon as possible to get checked out. My doctor sent me down the hall to the OBGYN office for an emergency appointment. The OB doctor asked me several questions and I gave her the paperwork from my doctor. The OB doctor examined me and said everything was fine but told me to make an appointment with the specialist for an ultra sound. She gave me a packet about pregnancy and being a new mother and sent me on my way.

Even after not getting any fertility treatment the good LORD saw fit to bless us in a mighty way. A new life inside me: a child for us to love and raise. I called myself a barren woman for several years. I thank GOD so much for the miracle. It was time for my appointment with the specialist. More blood tests and more urine samples. She said everything was normal. She made an appointment for me to come back in three days to get another ultrasound. At this appointment, the doctor told me what to expect in the days and weeks ahead. The doctor took pictures and then it was time to hear my baby's heartbeat. Wow, my miracle and my blessing. I wish my husband could be here. Yes it was time to hear and see my baby. I saw the head and the almost formed body: so tiny so precious so beautiful. I love you, I love you already.

The strong fast heartbeat was echoing through the room and my baby was positioned upside-down, which is normal. All babies are upside-down for most of the nine months or until they decide to move on their own. The specialist said I am six weeks and the fetus is the right size in the yoke sack. The heart is strong and all is well, very good. It's time for you to go to a regular OBGYN to get started on prenatal care and vitamins. The specialist prescribed progesterone to be inserted into my birth canal to help maintain a healthy pregnancy. The doctor gave me two pictures of my beautiful baby in a frame and said "good luck, Fatimah". I was so happy I couldn't wait to tell my husband the good news.

That weekend my husband surprised me and we went to a cabin in the mountains. It was beautiful up there, peaceful and very relaxing. We watched the sun come up and go down. We really enjoyed each other's company and vowed to do this again, soon. In the back of my mind I felt at peace and I wanted to be careful about the baby. My pregnancy was high risk. I felt so special so blessed. As the weekend came to an end we prayed thankfulness and for traveling mercies: it was time to get back to reality.

The next month my husband and I went to the new OBGYN for a checkup. The doctor was very nice but her office was different from the specialists' office. She didn't require any blood work from me, she wanted to do an ultrasound first. As I climbed onto the table my heart raced with excitement. I couldn't wait to hear my baby's heart beat and see the tiny miracle inside me. The doctor started the examination and right away she said she could barely hear the heart beat and that it was very faint. I complained about her equipment because my baby was fine prior to the visit to her office. I could feel my baby everyday inside my stomach. The feeling was not my own. I have a beautiful child inside me alive and well and I have pictures. I shouted your office is old and your equipment was outdated. I complained the whole time I was there. Why is it that her ultrasound machine could not pick up my baby's heartbeat or movements? My baby's heart was beating loud and strong before. I am eight weeks pregnant. I have pictures. What is going on right now? My husband sat there in silence as his eyes were staring at the monitor. I insisted my baby is fine and the doctor's machine was so outdated that it is unable to send the correct information. My husband told me to calm down and listen to the doctor. The doctor looked me in the eye and told me the fetus had not grown and was not eight week size. The fetus was only the size of five weeks.

I did not want to hear what the doctor had to say. I felt she was wrong because I was in deep denial that anything was wrong. The doctor was frustrated and again told me to calm down. She said I was to go home and rest and coms back the following week for another exam and we will take it from there.

I prayed several times about my baby. I prayed with someone from the T.D. Jakes ministries and I prayed to the sky on my knees. I had been spotting for three weeks and that is not good. I remembered telling one of my friends I was pregnant and they did say "don't get use to it, don't get too attached'. What did they know? Anyway, I was already attached to the miracle inside me.

Later that week we went back to the doctor. She asked another doctor to examine me because I was already upset with her. The other doctor started the process and she could not find a heartbeat. At that very moment I lost myself and blamed the doctor. I told her I have pictures of my baby. The doctor looked at me and my husband and said "You are having an early miscarriage". Why did she say that?

Why did she say that to me? I don't believe her! I don't believe her! Shut up, stop saying that to me! Stop! They must have done something wrong! I read my prenatal books and I followed all the steps. What could have happened? My husband was silent but he understood what happened. Our child, our miracle was deceased. After I calmed down I got dressed and we went to the doctor's office to talk. The doctor explained to us how the fetus will come down on its own in a few days and not to panic but call her and then go to the hospital. After all that, they sent us home.

I was so dead inside. Briefly I actually felt what it was like to be a mother, to be pregnant. What a beautiful feeling impossible to describe. I had a miracle beyond all miracles inside me. A child from my beautiful husband and me but my time was up.

Labor Day weekend was coming up and I was still spotting. It was a quiet weekend at my house because I was waiting for the full miscarriage to take place. As the weekend went by all I could do is think about my baby. Who am I, what am I doing here. It was the worst weekend of my life, or so I thought. Well, it was Labor Day morning and I didn't want to get out of bed. I felt like a failure to my husband, our families and myself. I looked up at the ceiling knowing deep in my heart what was going on in my body. Looked at my husband and began to cry silently. In a way I was at peace as my baby's spirit was preparing to leave its body and mine. I looked at my husband again and I asked for forgiveness. Forgiveness for not being able to give him the family he wanted so badly. As I lay there in silence it was time, time for my child to leave me. That morning, my baby went up to heaven to be with the MOST HIGH. I knew exactly when it happened. I felt it, I saw my baby's spirit leave my body and ascend up to GOD. I watched the whiteness as it floated away. I knew what just happened. I prayed to GOD and said "YOU gave this baby to me and now I give my baby back to you, thank you, thank you Father for what I have felt these past few weeks, thank you.

I took a deep breath and cried and said "LORD I give you the child you gave to me". My baby was stubborn like my husband. After two long depressing weeks the fetus would not come down on its own. The doctor called and I told her the fetus did not come down. She immediately scheduled me for surgery to have the fetus removed for fear of infection. Soon they will take my baby from inside me. My sweet baby whom I wanted to stay. I pray that everyone forgives me for my failed task. I had a long talk to my husband and told him he was free to go. Free to leave me and find a woman who can give him a family and that I am sorry, but he chose to stay.

The 21st of the month came and it was time for the surgery to remove my baby. I was in so much pain that morning. I cannot describe the sensation. I could barely walk into the hospital. I couldn't talk to anyone, especially my family. I just stared into nothingness. I thought about my husband's family. Children are the cornerstone of their lives. I haven't been able to give my husband children for 14 years and counting. I asked myself "Would they blame me for what has happened"? I am so ashamed and soon to be empty. How will I face what is ahead? My husband says he is not mad at me, but is he? Into surgery I went and when I woke up I asked the nurse was my baby gone and she said yes.

My baby is gone. Yes, my baby was gone but I am not a barren woman anymore. I would rather my husband be mad at me then mad at GOD. GOD blessed us to conceive. GOD would never put more on us than we can bear. GOD knows what we can and cannot handle. I know this was a sign. We need to change, change for the better. We need to get closer to GOD and each other so we can make it through this life's journey.

I cry all the time about my baby. My husband wants me to bounce back quickly and I am trying but it is so hard. Help me mommy, help me my husband and please help me GOD. I prayed and I prayed to GOD to bless us again, to give me another chance.

I have my baby's picture, I need it. Approximately 2 weeks after surgery I had to back to the OBGYN for a checkup. I don't know why there was nothing to check but I went back with my head held high and my mind stayed on Jesus for peace. I cried at the appointment for the loss of my baby. I miss my beautiful baby. I am truly trying to heal for my husband's sake. I hope I don't disappoint him as I already have. I miss my baby, I miss my baby, I miss my miracle. The pain of the surgery lingers on. How long will this pain last? How long will I hurt?

One day while I was praying for peace and acceptance the phone rang and it was the doctor. She explained to me that the fetus had an extra chromosome and that is what caused the miscarriage/death. I exhaled, I was not the blame, it was not my fault. I did nothing wrong. It was not my fault. My baby was gone, but I am not a barren woman anymore.

I remember having encounters with messengers since 1994 but I don't remember if I received them before that date. In 1995 I started listening to them and writing them down. That year the Lord sent a stranger to my workplace; in a very bad part of town. The area was known all over the state as extremely dangerous 24 hours a day with drug addicts, homeless and the mentally ill wandering the streets. There were drug addicts and a lot of crime on every corner. There was blood on the streets and all over the sidewalks. I remember getting off the bus one day and practically stepping in a fresh pool of blood running down the sidewalk. I almost got back on the bus. I was so afraid but I needed to keep the job. I wanted to work so I had a job to do. On January 20th I got off the bus as usual and was on my way to the building, a stranger walked up to me and said "You are diligent, you are needed by the men inside and outside this building. The homeless men and the drug addicted men respect you. You are not working for this company, you are working for GOD". The stranger walked away and I never saw him again. I walked into the building in silence and quietly said "Thank you LORD". I changed a little that day and it was good. As the days turned into weeks which turned into months, my fear turned to compassion and my heart was sad for the people. I suddenly wanted to make sure they all got the help they needed. GOD's love was inside me and I didn't even know it. GOD's love feel's warm and makes you smile, makes you laugh and makes you cry. Whatever I can do, I will do with GOD's help.

On March 15th, again on my way to work, a stranger had a message for me from the LORD. He said "your work here in this bad area of town is almost done, you have worked diligently and you should be thankful. The men have been betrayed for years by your bosses and coworkers. You have helped them and you have worked diligently although it will be ending soon". The stranger bowed his head as I walked pass him and I praised GOD and went in peace.

These messages help me through my journey in this life. I thought to myself: the Lord speaks to me through strangers. That is such an honor, so very special. I was chosen to change an atmosphere. Who is worthy of so much? What some of us see as divine intervention, others see as coincidence. Divine intervention always wins in my book. GOD has the whole world in His hands.

Through the entire summer of 1995 strangers were sent to me for help and messengers were sent to me with messages from the LORD. Some people would come up to me and say boldly "You are a Christian aren't you"? I would just look at them and smile. By the grace of GOD I was willing and able to help. If I run into an obstacle I would look to the hills from whence cometh my help because my help comes from the Lord: the one who made heaven and earth . . . . Psalm 121:1-2 vs1 "I will lift up mine eyes unto the hills, from whence cometh my help. Vs2, "My help cometh from the Lord, which made heaven and earth". (KJV).

I had joined a church not long after and one Saturday morning they had a Prayer Breakfast. I didn't have a heavy spirit that day. Shortly after I arrived, I received a message from the Lord. A woman (whom I did not know), came up to me and said "You have the spirit of praise". I stood there in shock and could not speak. I thought to myself, "I have what"?

Do I even know what Praise is or how it works? I had to sing that day and I sang my heart out in the crowded fellowship hall down stairs in the small church. I really didn't understand the full concept of praise. How could I have that spirit? I just chose a song that I liked. After I sang, the woman came up to me and repeated what she said earlier. That day I kept singing, it was like I couldn't stop singing. I don't remember how I felt through the events of the day, no, I don't. When I left the small church I was somehow a little different.

Several years later I left that church and joined another. This church was nice and closer to home. They also had a Prayer Breakfast program that was held in a big white banquet room. Everything was white: the tables, chairs, walls and the floor. The music started and it was good. The speaker spoke and she was awesome. I remember standing to my feet several times. I cried, laughed and sang songs of worship. The evangelist that brought the message was very fulfilling. It was a long and wonderful day. As I was leaving the big white room I had an encounter with a messenger. The woman stopped me in the stairwell and said "You have something inside you that has not yet matured". When it does mature, you will give birth to it. It is not a child/baby, but something else. It is growing inside you but not yet matured. Don't worry about it; it will not come out until it is time. You will give birth to it, you will birth it out". I stared straight into the woman's eyes. The words she said cut right through me. It was like I stepped out of my body, like she could see right through me, inside my soul. I guess she could.

One day I went to get my tire changed in a little shop in a town called Pine Lake. I was feeling at peace that day and there was much joy in my heart. The sun was out and the birds were singing. The wind was blowing ever so slightly. What a beautiful day the Lord has made. A man walked toward me who looked like he was in need and had a peculiar expression on his face. I said hello to him and I he asked me for help: financial help. I said ok or something to that effect. I told him I would be right back. I went inside the building to get change so I could give him some money and when I returned the man was gone. I asked everyone where he went and they all said "he went down the road, don't worry he is here all the time, he will be back". I thought to myself "Oh no, how am I going to give him some money"? After my tire was fixed I waited in the parking lot hoping the stranger would appear in the distance, but he didn't. I waited quite a while and then went to the person who worked on my tire and asked him to give the money to him when he returned. The man said "Ok". He looked in my eyes and asked "Are you an evangelist"? I smiled, then turned and walked to my car.

I was remembering and writing, writing and remembering, such an experience to behold. While writing this page, I stopped in the middle and wrote a song. I guess it was a song. That sort of thing has happened before during the course of this experience. It is relevant? Time will tell.

It is a very powerful and awesome thing to be able to call on Jesus in your time of need. We always learn lessons when we are not trying. This particular time I believe fear and frustration made me remember that when you call on the name of Jesus, every knee will bow and demons will run far and fast screaming their lungs out.

I was at work one day and the place was filled with all kinds of spirits. There were happy spirits, sad, angry, hopeless, helpless and anxious spirits. I went up to the intake window to see why this man was so angry and troubled. He seemed like he really wanted to hurt someone, namely us. When I got up to the glass I looked at the angry man and as soon as I got eye contact I whispered "Jesus". The man turned and ran out the door and up the street screaming! I watched him: the demon ran for his life. The people stood up from their chairs and asked me "What did you say to him"? I just smiled and walked away. I was stunned myself but thankful we were all safe. I thanked GOD several times and was at peace the rest of the day and night. We have power to tread on serpents and scorpions! Luke 10:19 "Behold, I give you power to tread on serpents and scorpions, and over all the enemy: and nothing shall by any means will hurt you". (KLV)

I like many others have had a problem with backsliding. One time I was wrestling with my conscious over some things in my life and I started drinking alcohol again. My husband was all smiles and still hanging out and partying to no end. I had stopped but, was still fighting the feeling and one day I got weak. I then turned to an old familiar friend: E&J Brandy. I started buying bottles all the time. I don't know what came over me. I don't even know how many weeks I had been drinking before this encounter with a messenger came. I rode the same bus from the train station home every day. I passed many stores along the way. One of the stores sold alcohol, all kinds.

One day I got off the bus, walked into the store and purchased my bottle of Brandy with a smile on my face. I was living for the moment. I didn't care about the present or what would happen in the future if I kept this up. I was just living for the moment. Although I had been drinking for quite some time, this particular time I felt a little desperate almost anxious. After my purchase I caught the first bus going my way. The bus was very crowded. I thought to myself, "Wow, am I going to have to stand up all the way home"? I searched for an empty seat. I found one near the front. It was the only empty seat on the bus. I sat down and looked around the bus at all the people. I like to look at people. Their faces are very interesting to me. I thought to myself, "I can't wait to get home to relieve my stress".

I stared out the front of the bus and when I turned my head back to the middle of the bus a woman was sitting beside me. She was middle aged and had on a long black coat (remember all the seats were filled). I looked at her and said to myself, "Where did you come from"? The strange woman leaned over and whispered to me "You better get back to where you were, you better get back to where you were or it will be much worse, much worse". My mouth dropped open and the bus went silent. It was like I was in a tunnel of some kind. The only sound I could hear was her voice whispering to me and me thinking, "I know what she's talking about". I have it in my arms right now. It was at that moment I knew the LORD had never left my side. That HE still cares about me and loves me unconditionally after all the things I have done in my life and believe me, I have done a lot.

Okay!, okay! I screwed up, but, I was pulled back into the fold of life. Thank you Father. I can breathe because you LORD released the power to save **me** from the fowler's snare once again. I praise GOD! GOD loves me! Why do we find it so hard to believe that GOD's love is unconditional? I cry sometimes when I praise GOD because I remember the old of days and I am so thankful. It's like the song goes: "If I had ten thousand tongues, it wouldn't be enough to say Thank you LORD!

As we travel our journeys in life, we have encounters with messengers that answer to envy and strife. I know I am different and at some point in my life I had to accept and embrace that fact, But it was not easy getting there. Singing in a Southern Baptist Choir is no joke. Although I loved every minute of it, others asked themselves "What is she doing here, she is clearly not one of us, where is she from"? The self-appointed leader of the choir pulled me to the side one night at rehearsal and said "Do something about your hair", "Where are you from"? "You don't sound Gospel to me"? I was so surprised. I never expected that. I replied "I always wear my hair braided and I am from Pennsylvania". He turned around and announced it to the entire group. Some of them looked at me like I was dirt under their shoe. I thought I was seeking refuge in a safe and loving place but, no! I guess that's why I was left alone to walk down the long dark street to the bus stop all by myself every week after rehearsal. They didn't like me because I was different. Rehearsal was over and I was usually offered a ride, but not tonight. They all stared at me as they drove by me safe in their cars.

That night I cried all the way to the bus stop. I cried on the bus and I cried when I arrived at the train station. I was all alone and it was very, very dark. I paced up and down the walkway at the train station thinking hard. I was mad, sad, pissed off, angry and frustrated all at the same time. I looked up at the dark sky and questioned why I even went to rehearsal or wanted to sing for that matter. Then I shouted "I will just stop singing and I mean it"! That night would be the last I would ever sing. This was to be my final curtain call. I paced and I paced and I made up my mind that I would never sing again. I also vowed that I would never go back to rehearsal. I was hurt I thought, beyond repair and I continued to cry.

It was getting later and later and I paced and paced up and down the walkway. Where is the bus? Where are the people? Why am I the only one here? I told myself "I won't have to go through this anymore". "This is my last night doing this". With my back turned, I felt someone's presence. I turned around and a stranger walked toward me. He had on a long black coat and his hair was curly. I could not see his face because it was so dark that night but, I wasn't afraid. I wandered where he came from since I was the only one there. He stopped approximately two or three feet from me looked into my eyes and said "Do not ever stop singing, people need to hear you, you have a gift". "Do not stop singing". As the stranger was speaking to me it was quiet and warm and nothing else in the world mattered to me. How did he know what I had been through that night? Still crying, I told the stranger "I will not stop". I was crying so hard, that is all I remember him saying. Time stood still. I was stunned. I dropped my head and then looked to the sky and the stranger turned and walked away as if to vanish into the night. The stranger, messenger, well I never actually saw his face, only his short curly hair and his long black coat.

After I gathered myself I said "Wow, I am not supposed to stop singing no matter how challenging it will be, I am not supposed to stop". Who am I that GOD is mindful of me, that He hears me when I cry"? I looked up to the dark sky with bright stars as the wind blew across my face and thought "My purpose, my calling I know what it is, I am supposed to sing GOD's message to those who need to hear". What a blessing to know GOD is right beside me at all times. Thank you, Father. I love you too.

I have always questioned my worthiness because I have done so many things in my life. To be chosen for a specific, obvious purpose is truly a sacred blessing.

As I continue to write my story, I get very emotional. I often wonder where I would be if the Good LORD were to stop watching over me. In the pits of hell, that's where. Thank you, Father, I love you.

Being home alone at night or overnight was very challenging for me. I know it is because of fear. Sometimes I would hear things or I would see shadows and have all kinds of crazy thoughts. Not often but, when it occurs I have to get out of bed and anoint my house with Holy Oil. I know that no one and nothing can separate us from GOD's love. This particular night I thought I was having the best sleep in the world until a dream cane across my subconscious.

Was it really a dream or was it real? Well, this is what happened: I felt like I couldn't breathe and started gasping for air. I opened my eyes and looked around my bedroom. As I scanned past the television, I saw what I thought was a demon standing in front of the television set. The way it was staring at me was causing me not to be able to breathe. It was like it was telling me to die. I struggled for a moment telling myself to breathe and then it hit me: call Jesus! At first I couldn't open my mouth but I kept trying and thinking, "If I could just call Jesus, I would be saved". There was no sound coming out of my mouth, why? Finally, I was able to open my mouth and I called out to Jesus. Over and over again I cried out "Jesus! Jesus! Jesus! Jesus!" The calling out to Jesus came out very loud and suddenly my breath was restored and the demon disappeared. I was so thankful and relieved. I came out from my sleep thanking GOD for saving my life. That night I didn't go back to sleep for several hours. When

I dozed off it was an hour or two before the alarm rang and I had to get up for work. A journey into darkness and then rescued by the light!!

Another night I had a very vivid dream, I was driving down a long and winding road. I was driving so fast the wind was blowing across my face and in my mouth. The feeling was carefree and relaxing. Suddenly I lost control of the car I was driving and went over the roadside cliff. I remember looking to the left and looking to the right as I was soaring through the air not really grasping what was happening. It was like I was flying.

In the distance I saw houses and then I got scared because I was going so fast and realized I was no longer on the road. The car was still going forward but descending fast. Approaching below was a concrete wall and it was getting closer and closer. I screamed to the top of my lungs and then "BOOM", I crashed into the wall. I sat there screaming looking around and wondering what was going on. I cried "Why, Why?" I thought "I am never going to see my family, my husband or my friends, why"? I screamed to the top of my lungs and cried and cried because I knew I had died. I cried out so loud in my dream that the sound came through my sleep. My husband heard me crying hysterically and tried to wake me up. He kept calling my name and saying "Wake up, wake up".

I finally woke up crying and shouting "I died in a car crash in my dream"! I was a mess. My husband calmed me down and I laid there reflecting on what I had just been through. It was terrible. How do you recover from a dream like that? What did the dream mean? Was I going to die in a car accident?

It bothered me so much that I had to find out the meaning of the dream. This is what I found. (1) "Your beliefs, goals and life styles are clashing with each other". (2) "Your old life is dead and you have to shed the skin to make way for your new life". How profound, I understood the meaning. I was astounded. It's all about my new beginning. I am seeking GOD's face to grow spiritually so I can continue to hear from GOD. I want to receive understand and obey the special messages every time they come my way. I want GOD to always fight my battles and I want to always be obedient to GOD.

I was shedding the old to be able to grow into the new: obedience, faith, joy, love, peace and His presence.

That's where the book comes in. It's all about being obedient to GOD. I ran and ran from writing this book for more than twelve months. I kept getting messages and having encounters with people who knew nothing about the book asking me about writing the book or telling me to write the book. Finally, I gave up and surrendered to the deed. Like Jonah and the whale, I was afraid. I asked myself many times "What would I write about and would it make any sense"? I questioned my thought process. I doubted my ability to do such a thing. The encounters from the messengers about the book were coming from everywhere. Strangers and church members alike who knew nothing about the book and the struggle just to get started writing. I fought writing this book and tried to ignore it several times. But, it was impossible.

One Sunday at the end of service the Pastor called for alter prayer. I was led to a visiting Evangelist so I went up front for prayer. She prayed for my success at work and for my promotion. She said I am an entrepreneur on my job and she prayed for my book to be a success. I immediately started crying when she mentioned the book. Divine intervention!! She ended the prayer by praying for me to have courage and wisdom for what was to come. I opened my eyes and she was done. She hugged me then she asked, "Are you writing a book"? I said "Um I don't know, I guess so, I write songs and music but." Then I stopped talking and smiled because see looked confused and she said "Well, ok." I went back to my seat thinking here is that book thing again. I have to do something about this. Me write a book? How, when, about what? Then I said "Ok, this is serious, I have to do something". "I have to start writing, I will start writing".

I lead a lot of songs at my church and I welcome the Holy Spirit to get me through it. On first Sunday we have Women's fellowship. This Sunday we had guests that attended. A guest came up to me and said "You really mean what you sing, you have a fire inside and I see it on you". I looked at her stunned and blank faced. I smiled, Praised GOD and waked away. I said to myself "Someone felt what I was singing and they see something on me in spirit". "Thank you Lord"!! All I want to do is Your will for my life.

The children's department at our church asked me to write a couple of short plays and songs for an upcoming program. I was happy to help them out and it went very well. A teacher from the children's department from Green Forest church was there that Sunday and saw one of the skits I had written for our children and asked me to write something for her children. She called the theme "Believe, Achieve", I was so inspired I began writing that day. I wrote an interactive song so everyone could join in once the children started singing. I was excited about the song, it made me feel good. A few weeks later I saw the teacher from Green Forest and she was happy to see me. Her eyes lit up and she shouted "Hello, thank you for your anointed writing for the program, even the Pastor was singing along with the children, it was wonderful, thank you, thank you so much"!

She brought the program to show to me. It was nice. I was so thankful to the Lord for giving me inspiration to accomplish such a great task. With the help of our Father, I can do all things. What a wonderful feeling! Thank you LORD for blessing them and me!

A couple of weeks had gone by before I received another message. It was December 20th and of course I had not started writing yet. I was very stubborn. I felt like I had to get ready to write instead of just writing. Anyway, when the Deacons and Ministers went up to the front of the church for alter prayer (as intercessors), Shalesia caught my eye right away. I looked away and she caught it again. I was hesitant about going up for prayer. I guess I knew in the back of my mind what to expect: A message from the LORD. I sat there and prayed for others sitting in the pews and when I got done praying I looked up. Shalesia was standing there with her arms out stretched as if to say "Come to me, I am waiting, I am here to help you". It was as if she was waiting for someone to help, heal, encourage or bless in Jesus' Name. Do you know how powerful it is to have our arms out stretched to receive people sincerely? To see the power that came from her face, her soul. It was truly gripping. I felt it so strongly, it went right through me. I was overwhelmed and wanted to cry.

It is a true and wonderful gift to be sincere in intercessory prayer for others. The look on her face and her arms out stretched with the Holy Spirit inside her being. I thought to myself "Will she have a message for me; am I supposed to go to her"? Now I was standing but sat down again smiled and turned away. This time I prayed for my family and friends. As alter call prayer was coming to an end I looked up and down and up again. I couldn't fight it anymore. I went to her for prayer. When I put my hands into Shalesia's, she was silent for a moment. Then she took a couple of deep breaths closed her eyes and leaned her head back just slightly. When she spoke, her words turned into a message from the Most High. She began praying for my strength and wisdom. She prayed that I go where ever I am led of the LORD. She prayed for my courage. She released my hands and took my arms and said "I don't know what the LORD wants you to do but, you have to do it". I stared at her in silence as a tear rolled down my cheek and I trembled inside. I knew what she was talking about: The Book. At that moment I realized that my future really is mapped out and I can't get around it, I can't go under it and I can't go over it. I have to go through it and see it to the end the very end. What did I do soon after? I started writing.

On December 26th I received a text message form a choir member that said "You have to see 2010 before you can see 2010, please receive it". The message came from Kahlil. I know what he was talking about. I have to see my future vision as I gain wisdom and knowledge through spirituality. As I seek the Lord I grow. I must do and be in the will of GOD. I must be prepared for what is to come and I must be humbled to what I have been through. I have to see before I see. I have to see 2010 before I see 2010. I have to see before I see! Discernment!

Being unemployed was a very lonely, desperate and agonizing place to be. I went through so many changes at that time in my life. I cried most of the time. I felt like I was not a part of daily life.

I felt depressed angry and confused. I went to every job fair and applied for every job, weather I was qualified or not and nothing happened. Not one place called me back. I grew closer to GOD at that time and that was a good thing. I also wrote a couple of songs. I think all that was happening to me has prepared me for now. We have struggles because of bad choices we made in our past. So, yes, I grew spiritually and became so thankful for what I have. I talked to GOD about our home and our possessions. I said "LORD I know you didn't give this to us just to take it away". I cried and I cried and I talked to GOD more and more. At times I laid prostrate on the floor or would be on my knees: praying, talking, complaining and praising GOD about my situation.

During that time, I read the books of Job, Jeremiah, Psalms, Isaiah, Lamentations and some others. In a way I was still distraught because I was not bringing in any money (we never missed a meal), but I knew it was a hardship on my husband. I kept trying and trying to find a job.

One day, I received information about the DOL in Tucker. It was a new place and sounded promising. I went to the location several times and filled out several applications. I always checked the job announcement board and nothing happened for me. I started to get discouraged. I decided to give it one more try and I went back again. I applied for a job for which I had no experience and was way out of character for me. By this time I was willing to do anything. I didn't care what I had to do, I needed a job.

I stood in line waiting to discuss my application and resume' with the person who was conducting interviews. I thought to myself "I know I can do this job, it will be extremely hard and I have never done this before but, that's ok because I will finally have a job". I was my turn. The interviewer seemed nice yet stern. He asked me several questions and I answered as intelligently as I could. He seemed a little bothered by my presence. He asked me "Are you an administrator"? I said "Yes, yes I am". He wrinkled his forehead and folded his arms and said "Well then, what are you doing here"? At first I was speechless and then I said boldly "I am here to get a job like everybody else". He told everybody to have a seat and then he went over the job description with us as a group. When he was done he pulled out some other paperwork and called us up to the desk one at a time.

Some he told to leave and he would be in touch and some he told to stay. Then it was my turn. He looked me up and down. I was nervous because I had no experience what so ever for this type of work. He began to speak and I was expecting to hear about my resume'. Instead he was a messenger from the LORD and I was about to have an encounter. He was going to prophesy to me right there where I stand. He opened his mouth and said "Only the Holt Spirit can fill your void, you have work to do and you have to be prepared so you will be able to help and minister to people. You have a grace on your life and you need to stop wasting time. Seek GOD first and all other things will be added and your other issues will be resolved". My eyes filled with tears and I said "Ok". It was like the world stopped rotating on its axis. I knew other people were there but it was just he and I in that space in time. I received his words, my message from the LORD, but he was not done yet.

He asked "What church do you go to"? I said "Salt & Light Truth Center". He then asked me "Are you diligent". I said "Yes, I am". He said "You need to pray for your shepherd. You are an administrator, you like a challenge and you like to try new things. You need to be prepared. People will be coming to you and you need to be able to help them. You must be obedient to GOD and you must pray". Then he asked me "Who do you sing for". I said "Anyone who asks". His eyebrows raised and he said "No, a singer is just a singer if they are not anointed by the Holy Spirit. Only the holy Spirit can fill your void. I am not talking to you I am speaking to your spirit. GOD has been talking to you, but you will not listen. He sent (me) this fool, to tell you what you need to know". I was crying and understanding that I was not there to get a job. I was there to get my message from the LORD. I was chasing something I was not supposed to catch. The LORD was grooming me, preparing me for something greater. When the messenger was done talking to me, he turned around in his chair and his back was to me as if to tell me to leave. I stood there for a minute crying. I knew why he turned his back to me. I was not there to get a job. I looked down at my resume' lifeless on the table. He didn't touch it. I had the nerve to ask him if he wanted me to leave my resume' and he looked at me as if to say "Why leave it, it is of no use to me".

I walked away leaving my resume' on the table. I cried all the way to my car. I felt like I wanted to run away and hide or find a place to pray and ask GOD for forgiveness for what I had done. I got in my car and I drove and drove until I came to a church in the town of Tucker. I parked in the lot and cried even more. I decided to go into the church and pray, but when I pulled the door it was locked. I ran to the side door and it was locked also. I was so upset, I cried harder. Why was the church locked? I wanted to get in to pray. What was I going to do? I got back in my car and called my mother: no answer. I called my sister and my niece and still no answer. Then I remembered my niece was moving today. While still crying my eyes out in shock and denial I drove to my niece's new house. I felt so exposed and then I remembered: GOD sees all and knows all. My life is all mapped out to GOD's glory and I was created to do GOD's will. This destiny was placed in me for a reason and I need to stop running and most of all stop wasting time.

I need to spend time praying and asking GOD to help me hear what is being said to me so I will know what I am supposed to do. I am one of the chosen! I was chosen to change the atmosphere!

When I found my family I was still in tears but had come to grips about the message I received, therefore I had calmed down. Everyone was glad to see me and thought I came over to help with the move but I was there to tell my story or seek guidance or something. I didn't know what. I guess I just needed to feel my family's presence. I told them what happed to me and they all said "Obey GOD, It's going to be alright". I started crying again and could not stop. My mommy hugged me and I was comforted. She whispered "Obey GOD, It will be alright". I took a deep breath and sighed with relief. I felt much better but still in shock from the events of the day.

I went home and prayed and cried and prayed and cried. This is what I did for several days. All I knew to do was to seek GOD's face, seek answers to all my questions and ask for forgiveness for not paying attention.

Before I knew it, it was January and Martin Luther King Jr's Birthday. I woke up that morning from a very peaceful sleep and I felt peaceful. I walked into the living room and was compelled to play a track of music I had for a couple of months. As I listened to the music, it spoke to me like never before. I cried and then started writing lyrics to the music. The words were pouring out of me so fast I could barely keep up writing them. The music was going right through my being my soul as if I were in the presence of GOD. I wrote a most powerful song of praise. It was then I was transformed into what I was supposed to be from the beginning. I was stripped down to nothing and I was bare to all. I sang the song over and over in praise to GOD, my Father the Creator. I am a child of the KING!

The song is titled "And I". It is a very powerful song of praise to GOD with testimony of where I am in my new (awakened spirit) relationship with GOD. The song and everything I write belongs to GOD. This song belongs to GOD, I am just the one who was appointed to write and sing it to my brothers and sisters who need to hear this message of praise and testimony. Here are some of the lyrics: "Just because I cry when I praise, I remember the old of days and I, and I, I praise you LORD, oh LORD I praise you. Take my hand and lead me to your place of peace". Yes, this song is very powerful.

When I was done writing the lyrics and memorized the melody I called Terry at Partee studios and my expression spoke for itself. I wanted to record the song right away. In two days the song was complete. Awesome is my GOD! I had a ministry engagement coming up that weekend and I wanted to minister that song. It was our church anniversary at Salt & Light Truth Center. I was supposed to sing a couple of songs and I wanted my new song to be on the list. That day I rehearsed for hours. I rehearsed so much I got a headache. Once again, I waited and struggled before I put the whole thing in God's hands. Why do I torture myself so much?

When I arrived sat the church I had the jitters. I was nervous and excited. I wanted everything to be right I needed everything to be right. I decided to rehearse again before everyone arrived. As I sang it seemed as though the Angels had arrived to hear the message. Peace and calm came over the room and it was once again as if time stood still. For that I was very thankful. After rehearsing, I took my seat because guests were starting to arrive. The program began and it was good. Then it was my turn. I was asked to tell a little bit about myself and to introduce and talk about the songs. I gave the crowd the basic information and background on my first piece called "Faith Walk". It is spoken words to music. As I told the guests where the words and lyrics came from I could feel the Angels in the midst. The music was cued and I opened my mouth to begin. The people really listened and shook their heads as if to agree with what I was speaking to music. Their eyes were big with wonder as I ministered in spoken word. They listened as Faith Walked through the room.

When I was done, they applauded heavily with claps and smiles. I humbly thanked the LORD and moved on to the next song. After catching my breath I introduced the song: "And I". I told the people I had written the song on the Martian Luther King Jr holiday (Monday) and within three days (Thursday) recorded it and now singing it to you two days later (Saturday). Divine intervention!!

As I started singing, I left my body. The angels were dancing for the LORD was in this place. Peace surrounded everyone. Tears fell from eyes in the audience, from my eyes and from my husbands eyes. Some people swayed in their chairs and others waved their hands in surrender. There was a deep silence in the room. They listened to every word of sincere and thankful praise I sang. My voice was angelic, my actions were fluid and my praise was from my soul straight to the throne. The atmosphere was blessed with anticipation and warmth and the blessing of peace was in everyone's heart. When I stopped singing, they applauded and I truly believe the angels rejoiced.

As I walked to my seat, I looked around and my husband was wiping his tears. Then I remembered the day I was told people need to hear what I have to say. I touched many hearts that night in January. The LORD blessed me in a mighty way. Towards the end of the night, Shalesia came to me and said "You are going to go far I can feel it in my heart. Always express like that when you sing and speak. Let yourself go, you are going to go far". I received a lot of complements that night. With each one I gave all the glory to GOD because by His grace I go. I will always praise GOD from the raising of the sun until the going down of the same. People seem to look at me differently now. I only want to seek GOD's face and let miracles happen. Be careful what you ask for.

A few weeks later, I was asked to minister at a party in Peachtree Corners: a secular party and we had a snow storm (very unlikely in the south) that night. I rehearsed that evening at home and my voice kept fading in and out. Needless to say, I was concerned. As I should have done in the first place: put the entire process in GOD's hands. So I said "LORD, if this is what I am supposed to do things will work out". Then I thought about what the messenger said to me that day at the DOL, "People need to hear what I have to say". So I got ready to go and decided to ask my husband if he wanted to drive me there. To my surprise and relief, he said yes. I was so thankful. My husband "Taheem" came with me and that was wonderful knowing he does enjoy the music and singing of the Gospel as much as I do. It was a blessing to have him there with me for support. I only wanted to be in GOD's will.

When we arrived, we were treated very well. The food was great and the other artists were very good. Time went by and then it was time for me to minister. I asked the LORD to remove me from myself and to use me for His glory. They introduced me, it was time. I was shaking and exploding at the same time. A sort of quickening in my spirit I guess because so much wanted to come out. I could barely walk to the center of the large ball room with the ministry inside me exploding to come out.

I was shaking from my head to my toes full of life giving ministry. I put the microphone to my mouth and I ministered in song and in spoken word. As I ministered I looked around the room at the people. Some were listening more than others. By the looks on their faces, some felt I was just too deep to comprehend. In some of their eyes I could see hope and fear and the LORD was in the midst. When the part I played came to an end, I received extensive applause. As the sound of clapping rang out I looked up and thanked GOD for the anointing to send His message tonight. The DJ looked me in my eyes and said "Wow, you did a good job tonight"! I smiled in silence and walked away. Soon thereafter it was time to leave and I had to say my goodbyes to the people. As I was walking through the crowd to leave, two men came up to me with their eyes full of hope and said "Thank you! Thank you for that word"! I smiled and replied "I give GOD all the glory and only by His grace". At that moment again time stood still and I realized that I was supposed to be there to deliver this particular message to those who were supposed to hear. I was obedient to the LORD and the LORD provided according to His riches in glory. "I thank you LORD for your grace and mercy"!

I am so thankful the Lord gives us power over the enemy. We have to tap into that power at all times. When we are persecuted for no good reason, only because those around us are pure evil, we do not have to succumb to those forces. I have witnessed and have been a victim of those forces more than once. When I am weak GOD is strong to help me overcome those evil obstacles. Although, at times we cannot get out of our human presence, we still have power to trample them in the midst of it all.

On several occasions I have prayed and anointed with oil many areas where there has been evil. I will not hesitate to do so at any time to get through the evil realm of things. GOD is not the author of confusion and promises in His word to give us power: Luke 10:19 "Behold, I give you power to tread on serpents and scorpions, and over all the power of the enemy: and nothing shall by any means hurt you". (KLV)

With GOD's word in me, I have been able to obtain peace where there is no peace and joy where there is no joy. It is truly a blessing to have such power over the enemy so we can live our lives the way GOD intended. When you anoint an area and rebuke the enemy/evil spirit, then the powers of GOD can open up within you to trample them. They become afraid and will not invade your space of peace. I have seen this for myself, even to this day. Once you anoint, the evil spirit will look upon you but will not harm you because of the power of GOD's grace on you. Please, you must believe this with your whole heart and soul and it will come to pass. Many people do not believe this to be true nor do they understand the power we have over the enemy. Therefore, they suffer needlessly in many situations. We must rebuke all evil that approaches us and we must tap into the power that has been given to us by GOD. We must live peaceful joyful lives as the LORD intended. Do not be discouraged when evil comes knocking at your door. Nor be discouraged if you feel overwhelmed when evil is near. Rebuke, anoint and call Jesus' name several times.

After this, you must believe with all your heart and the evil will run to the other side of the mountain. The evil spirited person will quiet down and peace will prevail every time. But you must believe and depend on GOD to make it so. You will see for yourself that GOD is all powerful and nothing by any means will harm you. Call Jesus' name, He is waiting and he will answer if you only believe.

One day I was attacked by an evil spirit for no reason but the spirit was in my midst. I wrote this message peacefully to the spirit: "I am not the cause of your problems; I am not the cause of your pain. I didn't make you regret your life and I didn't bring your rain. Stop blaming others for you misfortune and talk to the One above: the One who holds you in His hands, the One who created to dove, so close your eyes and remember to feel the love. The love that you really need is not in a person's spoken words and it's not in something you will read. Just know for yourself I am not the cause of your problems and I am not the cause of your pain. I didn't make you regret your life and I didn't bring your rain. Call only on the one who set the captives free: call on the one who you use to believe. Stand still and know who GOD is and then you can truly receive and then breathe".

In spite of all the things we have done in our lives, GOD still loves us unconditionally. We should be thankful for each and every day. Life! This comes to my mind "The wind blows and the grass it grows and the sunlight is in your eyes, wake up your spirits the LORD is calling and the others have said their goodbye's. Jesus, you are the open door, Jesus, there is no more, yet you ask and I wonder why".

At rehearsal we were introduces to a new song. The song is called "Everything" by Tye Tribbett. When I hear the title I was so thankful because the song speaks to my spirit. The song is how I feel about GOD. I was asked to lead the song and of course was more than happy to do it. I was nervous and happy at the same time because it is truly a powerful song. To sing to the Lord, You are everything to me is an honor a privilege and so very powerful. Would I be able to contain myself? Would I be able to be so sincere that people would accept the message with sincere gladness and thanksgiving? Would their spirits soar as mine while I am ministering in song?

I hoped for all those things and more, much more. I wanted GOD to be praised and worshipped with everyone's heart and soul. I wanted spirits to dance. I wanted joy and peace. I wanted so much. Rehearsal did not go very well at all. I asked the LORD to provide what was needed for this message to go forth. I rehearsed and rehearsed. I listened and listened. I meditated on the song over and over and I watched the video several times. I wanted this song to be in my bones. I wanted every fiber of my being to be wrapped around the words and music. I wanted to go to a higher realm in this song and the LORD provided all that and more.

When I opened my mouth it was quiet except for the music. I was trembling full of ministry. The Holy Spirit was preparing me to send this message in song to the ones who needed to hear. I sang and I sang and the angels showed up and the people were crying and praising GOD where they stand and sit.

My heart was sincere. My soul was bare to the heavens. The flood gates were opened and the LORD gave and we received. Everything in me was coming out in full force yet I was humbled. From the tips of my toes to the top of my head I was in the spirit. My true being, our true being and with every breath the words came. Thank you, Father. You are my Bread of Life.

We all know by now this book is by divine intervention. I had to be reminded every now and again that this is GOD's work, not mine. I belong to GOD and this is to further the works of GOD.

I had not written in quite a while, I don't know why. I guess it had been about a week or so since I had last written. A reminder to write came to me by way of the telephone. My husband was talking to one of his friends one night about various things when his friend said "Please tell your wife I said hello". Then my husband's friend's wife asked my husband "How's the book coming"? "She is writing a book, right"? Very surprised, my husband replied "Oh, it's coming along". My husband put down the phone and asked me "When did you tell Penny about the book"? I replied "I didn't tell Penny anything, I haven't talked to her in several months, almost a year"! We looked at each other and my husband continued talking to his friend. I thought to myself "Wow that was divine intervention". It was a reminder that I need to continue to write. I have been reminded several times.

The LORD spoke to me through Penny to tell me to get back to writing. I was not surprised because I was being disobedient. I truly love GOD and I am thankful He loves me more. Thank you Father!

The following Sunday we had a guest pastor speak at our service. When it was time for alter prayer I was drawn to him in anticipation of a message from the LORD. For some reason I felt he could pray for me and would have a message for me from the Most High. I waited until he was free and I went up to him for prayer. In hope and anticipation, I was wondering if I am doing what GOD wants me to do. The Pastor looked at me and was quiet for a few seconds. He began to pray over me. I felt the Holy Spirit coming upon us. The Pastor was silent again and then he said "GOD wants you to be perfect in Him. GOD wants to lead this church in a praise spirit. GOD will give you the provisions for the vision to go forward". I must have thought for a split second "How", because he said the lord will give me the provisions. Then the Pastor said "The provisions will be for His work to go forward and not for you". I began to stir inside and tremble outside. The Pastor was silent again and then he said "Do you feel that"? "That is a release, a purging out of all that does not belong in you". Do you feel that"? "It is a releasing". A releasing"! I looked at him and a tear fell slowly from my eyes and the stirring eased away.

Who should I tell about this? Do I tell my Pastor? Do I tell my family? Do I tell my friends? I believe I should tell someone. I guess the time will come when I am told who to tell, the ones who need to hear. The LORD is truly with me.

I have a guarantee the good LORD has this book in his hands. This book is to be used to further His kingdom, to educate, to bless others and to teach. I was chosen for a specific task. Me, chosen! I pray that I do GOD's will as I am supposed to do and I pray I remain under GOD's wings for eternity. Our precious LORD has taken my hand to lead me.

One of the things I strive for is to be able to hear GOD talking to me telling me to do something, say something or go somewhere. I want to always be conscious to hear the Holy Spirits words. There have been several times when I was told or led to do something or say something

and I was not obedient out of fear. When that would happen it would bother me so much. I am glad I have changed in that respect. I hope to be alert and able to hear when the Holy Spirit is talking to me.

Once I was supposed to pray for someone. I remember the inside of my stomach was burning so hot. Out of fear and worrying what people would think of me, I did not budge from my seat. That was a big mistake. It bothered me for at least two weeks. The very next time I was compelled or led to pray was at Bible Study. I was overcome with the chills and then the burning inside me started up again. I knew what I was supposed to do and this time I had to do it. I spoke to the group and said "Brian needs prayer and we need to pray for him right away". Then the Pastor said "You pray". Was I the one supposed to pray? I guess I was. I was shaking inside and out but I prayed. The words flowed from my lips and I felt the Holy Spirit's power over me in the sanctuary. It was if time stood still and the LORD was listening so He could answer. When I was done praying the stirring and burning in my stomach went away. The Pastor said "Wow that was powerful, Thank you". I thanked GOD for using me and I was obedient. I give all glory to GOD for things seen and unseen, known and unknown.

One year our church took a trip to Tennessee for a fellowship weekend. It was restful and relaxing and the weather was great. The Pastor wanted to have a choir for service our last day there (Sunday). Of course we had to have some rehearsals and I didn't like that idea but I went anyway. I had a bad attitude when I got to rehearsal because I wanted to be doing something else, anything else at the time. We rehearsed for approximately one hour and we were released. That is what it felt like to me as rebellion captured my very essence. The next morning was Sunday and the Pastor said a few words and we sang and my attitude was clearing up. We sang as we should have and we were anointed, yes anointed. GOD's grace fell upon us in spite of my rebellion.

When we were done singing we had a testimony session. I was compelled to get up and tell the people not to be ashamed to praise GOD freely. I told them my story of being ashamed to admit that I have a relationship and believe in GOD. I guess I didn't tell people because I wanted to make sure I would be accepted by everyone at all times. That's why I never went public about my life as a Christian. It doesn't matter to me anymore. Now I will shout it from the roof tops that I am a Child of the King!

Anyway, I denied knowing GOD so much that it started to bother me. I became afraid that on judgment day the good LORD would deny me and I would be left outside the gates of Heaven. I have grown and learned not to be ashamed, but to be proud and thankful that GOD loves me just as I am. I became thankful to be a child of the Most High GOD. Yes, it was a long road getting there, but I will shout it from the roof tops "I am a Child of The KING", and thankful to be claimed by the Most High GOD in all the earth, space, time and universe. Hallelujah!!!

Praying for others is something that just happened one day. As you read previously in this book. This particular time was the first or second time it happened: The stirring inside me, the quickening of my spirit overwhelming me. Now more than ever I am compelled to do so at certain times. It is a surprise when it happens. Fighting and trying to ignore the sensation is not an option for me. I know it is something I am supposed to do so I just do as I am led to whom I am led to. I pray I never lose that spirit inside me for it is truly a gift from GOD. I pray I am always used by GOD.

On our church retreat a member shared a story about there not being any peace in their home. There was a stirring inside me and I was compelled to pray for them. The stirring was so strong I began to cry as I walked toward them. I was overcome and I did not have control over myself. I knelled before them and held their hands. I prayed for peace in their home. I prayed and cried and prayed and cried and I did not stop until I was empty. Then a few weeks later one of the members I prayed for came up to me and said "They had the most peaceful week of their lives". I smiled and gave all glory to GOD. Praying for others just happened to me one day when the Good Lord saw fit to give me and others the blessed task. 'Thank You, Father"!

One night at Bible study I thanked Shalesia for bring there to pray for the women. I told her she was needed and we really appreciate her presence. She responded "I am honored to be chosen to pray for the women and I hope I give the appreciate prayer". I told her the words will come when it is time to pray for others. Ask GOD to speak through you and His will be done. She wanted to say something to me and I said ok. She said "I feel you have a strong ministry inside you. "I don't know

what it is your singing or your book but I feel it so strong". We hugged each other and I got the chills. I thanked GOD for the confirmation and for GOD using her in such a mighty way and also for my confirmation. Prayer is so strong. During alter prayer at church she has given me messages form the LORD and for that I am thankful. Like I told my friend Heather, "My prayer changes things, I don't know about yours". I know you have to believe to receive GOD's blessing no matter what it is.

Who can heal the sick and raise the dead? The LORD GOD Almighty can! Don't forget, there is nothing too hard for GOD. GOD can do anything but fail; all knowing, all powerful and all loving to us all no matter what. Who can separate us from that? Nothing at all, neither life nor death. My spirituality is very important to me. I hope I continue to grow for the good of my life and to further the Kingdom. Yes, we all have fallen short of the glory of God. Let's try to do better, as if our life depends on it.

I love GOD and I try to be obedient to His will and to his way. Being in spirit is a feeling like no other. You are on a higher realm than this present earth. All you feel is joy and nothing else exists. The joy I feel in that realm, I want others to feel. If you close your eyes and ask the Good LORD to wake up your spirit, you will feel the joy of being in spirit. You must believe to receive for all things are possible in Jesus' Name.

Our human side is very weak and always compromising in any and every situation. Our feelings and emotions come into play and sometimes we deviate from the agenda at hand. We judge blame and complain, we process breakdown and we build back up. Our minds wonder and our hearts are broken. We are stared at and we stare back. If we only just close our eyes, pray and ask that GOD's will be done and all will be well.

Do we understand our ways? No we don't. We all have someone we do not get along with in one way or another because of our attitude or theirs. We must pray our way through and ask GOD our fix our heart so we can be used in the process.

One day I felt an awakening of the spirit in a fellow singer. When I looked at her, her eyes were closed and she was calling on the Holy Spirit to meet her in song. She was sincere and her prayer was answered. The Holy Spirit came upon her and was present in the place. It was a wonderful feeling especially for me. That is what I want for everyone ministering in song. I want them to become more spiritual and less human. I want them to become one with the song in the process and not just sing the song. Later that day I told her I felt he spirit awaken and rise. It was alive in her. I hugged her after we talked and a quickening came through my body. I told her about the feeling I had inside me and she looked at me and said "Thank you, I appreciate you saying that to me". I smiled and walked away. I knew it was not me: it was the Holy Spirit speaking through me to encourage her to keep seeking GOD for continued growth spiritually. It was well with her soul, it was well.

Things happen and move only in GOD's time. Not in the time or space we want it to happen. We must be still and wait. We must be still and know who GOD is and ask for only His will in our life. We fall by the wayside every day and many times in the same day. It is very hard to die to emotions that are not supposed to be there in the first place. It is very hard to let things go that you think you need. You want to cry just as I do while writing some parts of this book. Dying daily is not an option it is a requirement. It is necessary if we are to be unspotted from the world. Many of us do not belong here. We are unique we are different. We are a peculiar people. We are children of the KING! The Most High! The Beginning and the End!

We were created for one purpose; to bless GOD, to reverence GOD, to praise GOD, to know GOD and to be a part of GOD. Why must our human/flesh battle with us so? I battle and I battle as I try to stay alive and my mustard seed of faith gives me the strength to survive another day as this unique peculiar person I am created to be.

The LORD calls our spirits to awaken from sleep and we must also help others to reach their highest of heights. Wake up spirits, wake up spirits! The LORD is calling. Do you hear the call of the LORD? Will you reply or respond? Will you even know what to do when you hear the call? We have to be ready. We have to be ready for what is ahead. I want to see a special glow in all the people I meet. The glow of the LORD and I want to have the glow too.

I was between doctors and when I went to my new doctor he stared at me and then smiled. He said "GOD is with you". I was surprised because he didn't know anything about me. Somehow I knew he was speaking the truth.

One day while pulling out of my driveway, a stranger (Jehovah Witness) came up to my car and said to me "GOD is working on you right now". Some people know who I am and I don't fully know who I am. I ask for GOD's forgiveness when I get weak and go astray from what I am supposed to be doing. I always ask for help to continue this journey I have been given to follow. I talk to GOD and say "There are so many other people out there who are better than me and yet You choose me to love and guide on this special journey". "Dear LORD, I am thankful for this and I ask for forgiveness when I disappoint you". "I need Your love to survive. I thank you Father for choosing me. I gladly do Your will and I try do my best to stay obedient to Your way. Praise is what I was created do and everything I am I lay at Your feet and cast onto You for Your yoke is easy and Your burden is light". Do we do that? Do I do that? No, most of the time we don't and for that reason we suffer needlessly.

One Sunday at church I was again led to pray for someone whom I did not know. I saw her from a distance and she was in such despair. As I went down to pray for her the burning inside me got stronger and stronger. So strong that it over took my every action. She welcomed me at her side and then looked at me in surprise as if to say "What are you doing here"? I smiled at her and took her hands into mine. I was not my own, I belonged to the Holy Spirit. I had no control over the situation. The words came into me and I prayed for her peace and healing. The words came out of me and I prayed for her peace and healing. I told her to call on GOD. I prayed for her to call His name. I prayed into her GOD is waiting for you to call His name. I said "HE's waiting, HE's waiting, HE's waiting, call HIS name"! I felt a quickening chill and burning become stronger in my body. The Holy Spirit is moving! The Holy Spirit is moving! While I was praying for the woman I began to breathe heavy and then she began to cry. We stood to our feet and I said to her again "GOD is waiting for you to call HIM, HE is waiting, HE is waiting, call HIM, call HIM"! As the prayer ended, I gasped for breath. I felt very weak for I had poured all I had into the woman just as I was led to do. I walked back to where I was standing and I felt so drained to the point I felt I would pass out. My spirit was soaring with joy, unspeakable joy.

When I arrived home later that day, I slept for several hours. I was exhausted from the events. The next week one of my friends came up to me and said "If you are led to pray for me like you prayed for the lady, please run to me fast: Run to me fast"!

I thought about the good LORD and smiled. I told her I did not know the ladies name and when it is GOD's will, well, you know. We laughed and parted ways.

As ministers of the Gospel we are always supposed to be ready to serve. I sang at a funeral as a favor to someone I have known only a few weeks. He needed a background choir. When I arrived that day everyone was already rehearsing the songs for the service. There were several songs to sing. To my surprise I was asked to lead one of the songs. Of course I was hesitant because I didn't know the words and had not meditated on the song at all. Although I had never sang the song before, I agreed. I heard the song many, many times and I loved the song. It was one of those old funeral songs. He told me the arrangement of the song and we went over it a couple of times. It actually went pretty good. The problem I had was I had no time to memorize the words. My new found friend and choir director told me to use the paper to sing. I was shocked but said "Ok".

We walked out to the choir stand and I thought to myself "Do I panic or do I know in my heart GOD will make a way". The other songs seemed to go by so fast and now it was my turn. The song is called "Going Up Yonder", an old traditional song for funeral's. The music started and I began the song in alto because I am a alto and we rehearsed the song in alto. The musicians were playing in soprano. I heard the soprano key but I ignored the notes and sang in alto because I was safe in alto. The musicians and the director looked at me and said "No, bring it up"! The fear in me really wanted to say "No, I am not a soprano singer"! I took a breath and closed my eyes and let go and let GOD. I sang soprano comfortably. The Holy Spirit was inside me and I sang and I sang. The people were on their feet. The director turned around looked at me: put his hands on his hips as if to say "Sing that song, Praise GOD"! I hit notes that I could never hit on my own. The people clapped and praised the LORD as the song came to an end.

"I give all honor to GOD". "Thank GOD who made a way out of no way". After the funeral the people thanked me for singing. It's true: I was supposed to go the funeral that day. I was so hesitant because we had an ice storm a couple of days earlier and the roads were covered in ice and snow. In the south we really have to wait until everything melts before we

fully function with regular day to day activities. I was very hesitant about going to help sing. But GOD . . . . is all I can say.

I was told I have the spirit of praise. I was told I have a strong ministry inside me. I was told I have prophesy in my spirit. Me. Wow, I am unique, peculiar and blessed!

One of my coworkers asked me "Why are you so nice all the time: so happy? Is it because you make 200k per year? How is it possible to be that way"? I was really surprised to get questioned like that. I really didn't think about what the other employees thought about me doing my job the way I do it. I just comes natural to me I guess. Anyway I replied "I believe I was born a peace maker and I just want everyone to be happy, joyful and have a song in their heart". "I really don't know how to explain it".

She then asked "Is it possible for me to be like that, to be all smiles? I just can't do it, I can't"! I replied "Everyone can be happy and approach life the way I see it and no, I do not make 200k per year. I wish I did but, I am thankful for what I do make. It is possible to be joyful and happy in life. Yes, my faith has a lot to do with it". Then she said "See you are not even cynical. Please bottle up what you have and write me a prescription"!

I was surprised about our conversation. I spoke from my heart. I thought about the conversation while at lunch that day. I thought I need to ask GOD for forgiveness because this joy that I have is only from GOD. I should have said that but I was hesitant. We all know what can happen in the workplace when you discuss your faith. That was fear and I should not have let that stop me.

I remember a visitor to our office came up to my desk and commented that I am so full of joy and peace and I am always smiling. He wanted to know what was inside me. I was surprised and didn't say anything at first but he did not move. I smiled and opened my mouth to say something and he said it for me. He asked "Is it your faith"? I replied "Yes, yes it is". He nodded his head and smiled. Inside I felt, I love GOD and GOD loves me. Thank You Father!

Another person said "There is a peaceful energy about you and you are one person I will remember. I can trust you, you are a sincere person. I don't know anyone else like you". "There is an energy around you that draws people to you. The same energy that drew me to you right now and I consider myself to have an attitude about myself. But you, I trust your energy"! I smiled silently and thanked the LORD. What was just said to

me was inspiring to me and helps me to continue to stay on the right path. Though it may be narrow, I will stay on it.

I was told that an ex-coworker resigned from their job because I was no longer there to work by their side. He had written a letter to the corporate office stating "When Fatimah left my side it was like the sun went down and the lights went out, it was unbearable". I didn't know I had such an impact on him. How was I supposed to know such a thing?

I ask GOD for forgiveness for the things I should know and don't seem to know. Like trusting GOD with every fiber of my being and never doubting that all is well. We fall by the wayside, but the Good LORD sees our heart and sees us in a different way than we see ourselves. The joy we have inside is truly GOD given. All the terrible things we go through and still have joy: to GOD I give all the glory and praise.

When you share what GOD has given you with people outside your realm, how do you approach them? While writing this book I knew how to approach them: **Ask for GOD's will to be done**. Fear always seems to play a part if you forget where your help comes from because this world is so different. You would think all would be welcomed with open arms, but that is not the case. Once we get past fear we can break through the barrier and do GOD's will as intended. Like when the person asked about my joy and happiness.

I should have blurted out "GOD is in me, I am a child of the KING"! Or do I meet her where I thought she was? Maybe she wanted to hear GOD's name or maybe she heard GOD's name without my saying it. It would be a blessing even for me that I may have blessed her.

The LORD works in mysterious ways and meeting people where they are is a wonder to behold. GOD met me where I was one day and for that I am thankful. People talk fire and brimstone, I talk peace.

The world has issues swirling around them because of people with various spirits battling. It says in Ephesians 6:12 (NIV) "For our struggle is not against flesh and blood, but against the rulers, against the authorities, against the powers of the dark world and against the spiritual forces of evil in the heavenly realms". Protect yourself, keep your spirits awake and talk to GOD every day.

The LORD has really blessed me over the years. I have no words to show appreciation. I know I am not worth all I have received. Let me

say again "I am Thankful"! You know the song: If I had ten thousand tongues, it wouldn't be enough to say thank you, LORD I thank you.

My journey thus far has taken me many places, seen many things and have been in many situations preparing me for this next leg of this race called life.

One evening while driving home from work I passed a church marquis that said "The Study of Angels". I got excited and wanted to be a part of the study. The classes were held at a church I had never been to before and I did not know if they would accept strangers. It was to be a six week exploration but I didn't care. I just felt I needed to be there in the midst of the study. I thought to myself "oh, Angels are going to be there"! The first night I went, I was so excited. The church was big and there were a lot of people walking around. I was a little shy because I knew people would wonder who this stranger is among us and asking themselves: What is she doing here? I walked through the crowd and I felt the people glancing at me. Most of them were much older and of course much wiser. I was silently excited about the whole thing.

I walked slowly toward the special room where the study of Angels was to take place. I looked around and the walls were covered with pictures from the bible. There were pictures of fellowship, holding hands and smiling. All the pictures were nice, but I still felt a little bit uncomfortable. When I finally arrived at the special room I sat in the back hoping not to be noticed. People sat all around me for we were all there for the same reason, the Angles. The class started. Although extremely excited, I tried to disappear and at the same time wanting to absorb everything that would be said and done. I wanted it all. I wanted the Angels to make their presence known to us. I wanted to see an Angel. It was time. The speaker came in the room. His hair was brownish white and he had on a dark blue suit. I was waiting in anticipation to hear what he was going to say. He introduced himself and asked the class if we believed in Angels. Most if not all of us said yes. Then he began to talk about the Angels in the Bible. I held on to my seat, my journey was about to begin. I tried to hang on to every word the instructor said about Angels. It was fascinating and enlightening. The people became very friendly and just as excited as I was.

The instructor told us Angels are all around us at all times. They are not seen or heard, they are watching over us and helping us. He also told us that to the very sensitive, Angels can be seen and heard. We all have encounters with Angels, although we don't know it. He explained the different kinds of Angels and their purpose as he understood. As the weeks went by, I felt alive and free in that class. I felt like I was actually there, in the midst of Angels.

What is an Angel? The definition varies and depends on who you ask and what you understand. Angel: A divine messenger of GOD or a guardian spirit. We all have them. I wish I had been a little more mature spirituality then so I appreciate the class even more. Maybe my eyes would have been open wider and I would have been more receptive to remember. I wonder, were some of my encounters with messengers with Angels? I believe they were, yes I believe they were. Thank You, Father!!

One night at Bible study we had a discussion about conflict. Actually, it was a spinoff of the Sunday sermon titled "How to Disarm Your Enemy". Usually at Bible study we discuss the sermon in detail and share our experiences relation to the topic. The Pastor Avery always says, "This is the culture of our church, here at Bible study: Sunday is just a taste". So, after the pastor lectures and we go over the scripture, we have discussions and ask questions. This particular night almost everyone had something to say. I understood because this was a touchy subject. Everyone was giving their testimony and explaining their situations and asking why they had to go through so much with coworkers or acquaintances. After each person would present their scenarios the Pastor would explain or elaborate to help them and us to understand how to handle their particular situations. I was listening very close and I could relate to almost everything being said. I was determined not to say anything about myself. I was determined to keep my silence and just listen. My plan was to only engage I the conversation. IF it is GOD's will of course I will share, but I didn't for see that going on so I was not going to speak.

As the evening went on I thought about many things and reflected on my experiences and what I had done to fight the battles in my life. Suddenly there was a mild stirring inside me. I thought to myself, "If this gets stronger I will have to speak, I will have to tell them my testimony of the power the protection the praise. My mind was racing and I still kept quiet. The stirring got stronger and stronger I couldn't contain it:

I couldn't keep my peace any longer. I finally raised my hand it got very quiet and all eyes were on me.

I opened with "I know this is going to sound way out there, but I am a witness to what I am about to say". I told them "If you want results, immediate results you have to pray and believe GOD will handle the situation". I would pray over oil and touch everything the enemy will touch. Go into every room the enemy spirit will go into, rebuke and pray: but you must believe you must totally depend on GOD to fight your battle. Anoint and touch your boundaries, the enemy spirit will not come into your space". When peace comes your spirit will soar with joy and you will realize how much power you have inside and outside your being.

Remember, we are spiritual beings living in human shells. We need to keep our spirits awake at all times. Once the enemy spirit recognizes or feels the presence of GOD, they fear that space. I have seen this many times. The enemy will run away from whom they are trying to torture. They stay away because they know they have no power over you anymore. The enemy spirit will hope in days to come that you let down your guard so they can come back and torture you again. Some of us let our guard down we all do at one time or another. GOD has given us power, we just have to tap into that power and wake it up. GOD's promise to us in Luke 10:19 "Behold, I give you power to tread on serpents and scorpions and over all the power of the enemy and nothing shall by any means harm you". You see, we all have power we have to tap into it and keep it alive. There are too many battles going on out here not to always have on your full armor. You know what I mean. The armor in the scriptures of Ephesians 6:13-17. The armor protects us from the fowler's snare: the armor gives us peace when we sleep at night; the armor gives us courage to stand up to the enemy spirit; the armor is a gift from GOD. Please tap into your power and keep it alive. Feed your spirit and stay alert, "For we battle not against flesh and blood, but against principalities, against the powers of this dark world" . . . Ephesians 6:12. If you believe, you will receive.

As I am writing this book, many have passed by glancing at me. They are curious and have asked "What are you doing"? "Are you writing a book"? I always pause, smile and wonder what to say to them. Why would they ask me that question of all things to ask me? Then I answer "Yes" and continue writing. They stare in amazement and yet only one person has asked me the title of the book. I asked him "Can you handle the title"? He replied "yes" and so I told him. It gave me chills to say it out loud and then he said "Wow, it means one thing and then another. It makes you think and it makes you wonder what the book is really about". I thanked him, he smiled and walked away. I thought to myself "This is divine intervention. This book is special, people will read.

A few days later another coworker (she is an Evangelist) saw I was writing. He asked "What are you doing, writing a book"? Again I smiled, paused and quickly replied "Yes I am". She smiled and said "Ok". She looked I my eyes and I felt compelled to keep talking I don't know why. Then I began to tell her about the book. That it was about my life. The messages and the encounters with messengers but was not specific to detail. She said "Oh, and how does that make you feel"? I replied "Well, I feel humbled going through this whole process". Then the strangest thing happened, I began to cry. She stared so deeply in my eyes I couldn't help but to cry. I covered my face and couldn't talk anymore. I thought to myself "Why was I crying"? Then she said "Oh, I'm sorry, I didn't mean to make you cry". She came up to me and hugged me and whispered in my ear "GOD is working on you; HE is removing things from you and getting you back to where you were before. Don't cry, don't cry its ok". She began to leave and stopped to turn back and said "You said things to me two years ago, but you don't remember do you"? I replied "No I don't". She turned and walked away.

  When she left I wanted to question GOD but I didn't. What was I going to ask? What was I going to say?

You can run and run for a little while but you can't hide when your time is up. I ran from writing this book for months and finally I gave in. I prayed and started writing. I began to understand my life does not belong to me. My life belongs to GOD. I am created for GOD and GOD alone.

  We do a lot of things in our lives, but do we do what we are ordained to do? Do we do what we are called to do by the creator? We can run and fight but we cannot hide from the fact that GOD has an agenda for us that we need to follow. We need to be obedient and surrender to so our lives will be manageable. Living in GOD's will mean's peace of mind and hope for you to do the right thing as much as you are humanly possible.

The elders have so much power when they pray. To be in the midst of them at church, wow. It's a different kind of atmosphere when the elders pray. Most people don't really pay attention when they play because we complain they pray too long or are long winded so to speak. The prayer of an elder is very powerful and anytime you can be in the midst, run for it. Make it your business to be there.

We were invited to another church to sing, sort of like a musical program. Toward the end of the service they called for alter prayer and all the elders came to the front of the church to pray. When they headed to the front I watched as each elder joined forces and locked hands as prayer worriers often do. I got an over whelming desire to be in the midst. The music was playing and the stirring inside was getting more and more intense. The elders started moaning and humming. My insides were burning with fire. Then the pastor asked if anyone wanted to join the prayer circle. I thought "Should I go or not"? I didn't want to seem too eager but I couldn't help it. At the last possible minute I exploded from my seat and made my way to the most powerful space at the front of the church: the prayer circle, full of elders sending up the most powerful prayers.

The spirit was high and my heart was throbbing with thankfulness. What was swirling around the elders was swirling around me. It was wonderful. It was a blessing. I approached the circle with expectation and anxiety. Expectations of answered prayer and anxiety of what it's going to feel like to be in the midst.

My hand gripped the person next to me I closed my eyes tilted my head back and took a deep breath. As I listened to the prayer I began to imagine myself as one with those around me. I always longed to be in a prayer circle full of elders, I don't know why. Yes I do, I wanted to feel the power it is associated with; I wanted to know what it felt like to have elder prayer wisdom flowing through my body. I was so thankful to be there in the midst of the elders praying: to have such a wonderful chance. I did not pass up that chance and the feeling, well, it was awesome!

The feeling I got from the whole experience that day was indescribable, humbling, needed, wanted, peaceful, tearful, empowering, explosive, blessed, blameless and beautiful. It was an out of body experience. My spirit soared above me to collect all the things I needed to survive so I can be empowered even more for the journeys ahead. LORD, You are Mighty!

Doors open all the time, but do we walk through them or are we afraid for fear of the unknown? Yes, that is the problem most of us have. You know the saying "Step Out on faith". Well without assurance or visual guarantee most of us are just plain scared. That's why we run until there is no place left to hide. Before we enter the 'Open Door", we must ask GOD if this is HIS will. Is this truly an open door in His will? Open doors are chances we thought we would never have. Open doors help to advance us in our lives; open doors are blessings of mercy to make the road we travel much easier to endure.

Tonight, I am invited to a book release party. I never thought in a million years I would be invited to a book release party. At first I said "Wow, I am writing a book this could be an open door for me. I am definitely going and it is in the neighborhood, yea". As the time got closer I started doubting weather or not I should go. I thought "Maybe I would have to buy the book I cannot afford or I could just enjoy the festivities. Then again I really don't feel well, I don't have any business cards and I need something to eat". Basically, I am making excuses out of fear and nervousness. Why? Ok I will go and be myself. I will let my light shine and maybe something will come out of this whole thing and maybe not. This will be a new experience for me. I have never been to a real book signing before and this author already has four books under his belt. I have nothing to lose yet everything to gain.

As the time drew nearer I decided to go. I remember when the stranger told me "Things have always been given to you". Is this one of those things being given to me? Do I question the situation or do I just go with the flow? When I enter the party I will ask GOD for discernment and then I will know if I am in the right place at the right time and if this is divine intervention or something else. We all know everything happens for a reason. There is a reason for this and I am going to go through this open door. So come what may and by GOD's grace I go. This will be a new experience like most things I have encountered lately.

I walked into the room and it was empty because I was so early. I met the author mid-room and he smiled. He welcomed me and thanked me for coming. I was nervous and reserved at first. I walked up to the book signing table and it was beautiful. I thought, "Oh this is how you do it". The evening went on and more people were arriving. Suddenly it became crowded very fast. There were cameramen filming other authors, photographers, movie producers, playwrights, singers, song writers and composers: so much talent in this room right now. It was so exciting. The cameramen were walking around interviewing random people and he came to my table. I was nervous again. What would I say if I were interviewed? My heart was pounding with anxiety. Then the camera man said "Hello, briefly, tell me your story". I took a deep breath and slowly began to talk about myself. I thought "Only tell the most important details or you will start babbling out of control". Things went well and after the brief interview I exhaled. I was happy I was approached by someone of significance in that sea of important people. After all the meeting, greeting, mingling, interviewing and eating, it was time for the author to get up and speak.

The author walked slowly to the front of the room turned smiled welcomed everyone and thanked us for coming to his book release party. He was full of wisdom and very friendly to everyone. He told of his many struggles. I hung on to every word. The table where I sat was occupied with two other women. One of which I was familiar with from our working in the same building. I found out later she was a singer with James Bignon. The other woman at my table was in the book were being debuted tonight. She went by the name of "First lady". We all introduced ourselves and talked as we looked through the pages of the book. I was fascinated. We asked the author questions and all was well. At the table we told each other about ourselves. First lady was an R&B singer and rapper in the past. She said that was all she knew because she grew up in that atmosphere. Then she turned her life over to GOD.

She became dedicated to the good LORD and now sings gospel music. She said she knew she had a higher calling on her life; to sing the Gospel, to sing of the good news of GOD. As she (First Lady) told of her past I began to reflect on my past. I remembered when my mother wanted me to sing gospel music and I refused. I remember winning the talent contest in high school and traveling with the drama club and my teacher "Miss Franks" to the city to see my first Broadway Play "West Side Story". I remembered getting mad as the new lead singer of a Punk Rock band and singing the wrong lyrics in front of hundreds of people. I remember not singing for such a long period of time that I lost my singing voice. My memories were a rushing river rolling over the rocks in the rapids of life.

So many things went through my head while First Lady was talking to us about her life. How she got to this point: she never gave up. She told us to never give up. She told us it is never too late and to never lose our dream and GOD is good. The things we go through to get to where we are today. I was almost in tears because there was my message. I was supposed to go to the book release party. This is divine intervention. I asked First Lady if I could reference her in my book and she said "Yes". Then she asked "Are you writing a book"? I replied "Yes, by GOD's hand and grace, I am".

We then talked about writing songs and writing music. She gave us some tips and we gave her some tips. It was a wonderful blessing for me. The whole night was an experience. I received my message and a free autographed copy of a wonderfully empowering book! Thank you, Father!

The journey of life is a delicate thing. Travel wisely so not to get stuck in the mud of confusion. I have grown to expect an encounter with a messenger or a message from the LORD in some form or fashion.

One night I was up pretty late watching TV. While channel surfing, I came across a Joel Olsteen broadcast. For some reason I stopped and wanted to hear what he was saying? He was talking about people not following their dream, letting them pass by and then finally listening to the desire to pursue their dream. He said that GOD instilled our dreams our calling in us and it is our obligation to go after them. We should feel the drive.

We should follow that drive and keep the fire for that drive and do not let that fire burn out. How powerful is that? Another message to encourage me to keep doing what I am doing and to pursue GOD's will for my life.

How many times, have we had to start over doing the things we are called to do because we lose our desire and our focus? That is not what GOD wants for us. At times I find myself losing my desire because of disappointments and then I have to pray and think about it constantly to get back on track. To get that burn back.; to get back to where I was before; to keep myself from going astray. Confession and humility are needed to get you back on track. I was really touched by Joel Olsteen's message and I believe it was by divine intervention that I stopped on that channel that night. I pray I never lose the fire, the desire, the drive to stay in GOD's will.

The dreams instilled in me by GOD are part of my soul. Your dreams instilled in you by GOD are part of your soul. You feel lost when they are not achieved. You feel as if something dies and you try to get it back to the way it was. To do that you have to think about it constantly and pray the Good LORD restores the blood flow in your veins; enlarges your territory and keeps you from harmful temptations. I was so thankful when I heard that message. That message relit a fuse in me that was trying to go out. The Good LORD always rescues us from ourselves.

We encounter messages from the LORD in so many ways. It is awesome to know GOD is mindful for us all the hours of everyday in foreverness. Does that make sense? Probably not, but you know what I mean. GOD loves us in spite of all we have done in our lives. Words cannot express how thankful I am to be loved so unconditionally. It is such a blessing. So much mercy and such grace from the Most High above all the earth!

One morning lying in bed I was listening to the radio I was feeling particularly strange about my life. I have so many things going on, I'm trying to do so many things and I'm trying to stay on the right path as I journey through this life. This message was for me. The radio personality said "GOD puts people in your path who are different and who bring something different to balance out what you are doing. What you have and can do is yours. What they have and can do is theirs and theirs alone. In other words, what they can do you cannot do and what you can do they cannot do". I thought "Wow that was so profound"! To hear my message at that moment in time and it related to what I was experiencing.

There have been a lot of people placed in my path throughout my life and all of them brought something different to the table. Balance; I never thought of that although it is necessary to go forward in the work we are doing by the grace of GOD. People are sent to us to work with us, to provide what we do not have. Knowing that helps me understand all the different avenues I am taking. It helps me to understand how and why I am meeting people coming from all different directions yet working for the same cause, GOD's will. Thank you, Father.

I dream quite often about many different things, places, people and situations. This particular dream made me so incredibly happy I was bursting with joy. I think about this dream a lot. I don't know if I was walking down the street or sitting in a crowded room. I really don't remember. What I do remember is how beautiful it was and how wonderful I felt at the time. Part of my desire is to help people find joy and peace and to smile in all situations; to help them to find real peace in their heart. I would love to heal them from their pain or ease their heavy burden with a touch or a smile. Anyway, where ever I was in my dream, I really don't know.

In my dream I saw a multitude of people all around me. I stretched out my hand and silver glitter sprayed from my fingertips as if to go forth to the people. Everyone the glitter touched they smiled with peace and joy. Everyone I saw I sprayed with glitter. Everyone was full of happiness. I smiled at everyone and in my mind I was saying "You can be happy, take some joy from me and feel the wonderfulness of GOD".

It was breathtaking and alive and the air was fresh and clean. It was truly an awesome thing to see everybody happy and full of joy. When I woke up from the dream, I thanked GOD for such an experience. I laid there in my bed and imagined what it would be like here and now if all of that actually happened. I took a deep breath and smiled in bliss knowing one day all people will live in peace and joy and everyone will smile at each other all the day long no matter what happens: one day Father, one day.

We are all messengers of GOD weather we know it or not. Some of us are used to help others to get to peace, real peace. Matthew 5:9 "Blessed are the peace makers: for they shall be called to children of GOD". Peace helps us get to happiness in good times and in bad times. Real peace and real joy is GOD given. For us to be used as a vessel we must first believe GOD's word, have a relationship with GOD and then you will receive the blessings of those who seek Him. GOD promises perfect peace, but we are so preoccupied with other things we forget the promises. Don't forget!! Remember to smile inside and know the way to true happiness and inner joy. I pray I am always used by GOD to direct people to peace, joy and happiness.

Yes, we are human and sometimes our emotions overtake situations. If we call on Jesus everything will be alright. Have you ever felt joy at a moment, unexplained and you smiled? That's God telling you He loves you He is there for you and you still have joy after all you have been through in your life. Please thank GOD in that moment, for it is the blessing of grace.

Most times in our humanness, we think about and tend to dwell on the past things we have done. These thoughts make us sad and empty of hope. Understand, GOD has forgiven us our past and we are restored to goodness. I do it all the time, I think about my past and feel I am not worthy of such goodness. I need to stop thinking like that, but my humanness keeps me in bondage when my thoughts go down that road of despair. All hurt and pain is gone, everything can change for you and me. We must believe His word and speak joy to ourselves and others to maintain the happiness we so richly deserve.

We all have struggles with many different things on our journey. I struggled with my church affiliation. I was a member of a couple of different churches before I found myself attending a nondenominational church. I was seeking the freedom to worship and praise the way I wanted to worship and praise. I often had to refrain from expressing myself fully because of the structure in those particular areas. After several years I often wondered if it was wrong for me to be there or was it time for me to move on. Am I in the right place at the right time? Is GOD's will for me here? Am I doing what I am supposed to be doing? Have I grown spiritually? If I have grown will I continue to grow here? Am I helping anyone along the way? These were the questions I asked myself.

At times I got upset and wanted to change direction because I felt I was on the wrong path. This actually bothered me for a couple of years. Then one day a woman who is very dear to my heart (we call her mom) came up to me and hugged me in fellowship. She then took my hands and whispered "You are a true blessing to me and my family as well as our church ministry. Your joy in the LORD is reflected in all that you do for HIM, which encourages so many others. We have had several conversations about you and how sweet, loving and caring you are. It is evident that the Spirit of the LORD works through you in ways that inspire others. I was led to share this message with you as I try to be obedient to the Holy Spirit. Be encouraged and don't be weary in well doing. Continue to trust GOD".

She turned and walked away from me and I was in tears. I was standing there frozen in time. Was time standing still yet again? It must be, I feel nothing but silence and peace. Tears continued to fall from my eyes as my senses slowly returned to reality. I felt such relief, like a burden had been lifted from my shoulders. It was a blessing to know that the LORD heard my concerns and answered them. I had no idea I was encouraging to anyone. I have the freedom to worship and praise GOD and I love it!

Sometime later after service a visitor came up to me and said "Do you remember what I told you when I was here before"? I replied "No, I don't will you tell me again"? She answered "You are very encouraging yes, yes very encouraging". Then she hugged me. I smiled and said "I give GOD all the glory"!

During alter prayer the following Sunday I was compelled to seek prayer from a visiting evangelist. I hoped she would have a message for me from the LORD. I went up to her she asked for my prayer request. I told her I needed peace. She reached for my hands and when I put my hands in her hands she began to pray. She trembled as she held my hands and asked God for my peace. She told the LORD I wanted to be completely His and I do. She raised my arms out stretched and prayed for removal. She again prayed to GOD that I want to be completely His. She prayed for GOD to see me through and to help me stay in His will, and that I cannot do it alone. I began to cry and then she pressed her hand on my stomach and said "It is done, it is done"!

She pressed her hands on my back, swept my shoulders several times and said "It is done! It is done"! The tears were falling from my eyes. I was so thankful for the prayer. I felt exactly the way she prayed for me. I do need help to stay on the right path. I do need help to fight the flesh temptations of life coming at me from all sides and I do get weak and weary.

When she stopped praying she hugged me so very tight with both arms and said "GOD is pleased with you and this is how HE is going to hug you". I was so thankful and so blessed from the message from the LORD. I really needed to hear everything she said to me: confirmation. Thank you Father! Thank you.

Messages come in all forms and in all fashions. They don't always come from face to face meetings with a stranger or someone you know. A message can come from something you see from something you do or from someplace you go. They can come in a song or they can come in a text. The most important thing is to adhere to the message and obey. You

will know whether or not it is real. Your relationship with GOD and your awakened spirit will tell you.

A radio personality sent me an email. It was a message and prayer just for me: divine intervention once again from the MOST HIGH. Thank you Father! This person was so correct it was shocking. I don't know why I thought that because my messages come in so many different ways. It seems when I start to lose focus on what I am supposed to be doing, I get a wakeup call or a reminder to tell me to get back on track. The message he had for me was as if he was talking straight to my face. It was like he knew what I was doing and what I was going through at that time in my life. In the email, he talked to me about faith in this season like he knew I was on a mission. He talked about hesitation, he knew I was hesitating. He talked about knowing the future and that was one of my worries. He knew all the things I had on my mind.

This is what he said "The seeds are planted and now it is harvest time. Pray for the following: Laborers to help with the vision and Wisdom to carry out the vision. Pray that the laborers sent are all on one accord. Pray for funding for the vision, Strength to see the vision to the end and God's perfect will be done". I read the message over and over again and to this day I read and pray about this vision inside me. This email really helped me to not worry about anything that has to do with this book. I was so overwhelmed with this book I felt like I couldn't get anything done.

Several days later I received another email. It was from the radio personality's wife. It was a message of encouragement to move on. She said in the email, "All of heaven is backing you". How powerful is that? Her message to me was very intense and uplifting at the same time. It was all about the promises of GOD to His children. She talked about focus and goals and how easy it is to lose sight on what we are supposed to be doing on our journey called life. She talked about the lost time in my life and that GOD will give it back. I wasted a lot of time and I felt it was too late to pursue anything meaningful. GOD knows our thoughts before we think. Awesome GOD!

She ended with several scripture references and told me not to worry about things. She knew what to say to me and for that, I am thankful. The Good LORD used a radio personality and his wife to send to me a message of hope and encouragement. With this message I gained reassurance from my Father in heaven telling me all is well and HE is with me all the way. We are not alone on this journey we call life. Our journey is special, sacred even, so we must keep going, it will be alright.

It is a humbling blessing to know GOD cares for us so much that He sends messengers to help keep us on track. I know now I must go forward with the task at hand, fight the good fight and never give up in the race. This race called with divine intervention, for I will bless the LORD at all times and HIS praises, yes His praises shall continually be in my mouth!

Messages from the MOST HIGH so special so clean: Messages from the MOST HIGH so peaceful so serene. If you are ever blessed to have an encounter with a messenger, know that GOD and all of heaven has your back front and sides from here to eternity.

Jubilee: Where unusual blessings happen. A jubilee is something to behold truly from your soul. How many of us have had unusual blessings? Normally we don't recognize them or we call it luck of the draw.

Blessings are what we think we deserve, but do we really? Are we living as we should or are we just living? Are we pleasing to GOD or are we pleasing ourselves and others? Do we have examples of unusual testimonies to share with others or do we just talk to boast about ourselves?

The stories I have told you in this book are testimonies from me and what I call unusual blessings, miracles and encounters with messengers of Divine Intervention. If your blessings are so off the wall or something you thought was next to impossible ("Knowing nothing is impossible with GOD"),I call that a miracle. The Good LORD takes care of us and we are blessed to have such a caring Father. Where would I be if it had not been for the LORD on my side? Where would you be if it had not been for the LORD on your side?

Through this wonderful and blessed experience, I have begun a new phase in my journey called life. GOD has been so faithful to me and my family; I hope I can at least come close to doing the same for GOD. I go into so many valleys and I have so many faults I get lost sometime in the doing. I don't know about you, but I will always need GOD's help.

I love You LORD, more than I can express. Your loving peace is sweet.

To touch the sky, to touch as one, this journey in my life has just begun. To the finish to the end I will run to the SON, for this race by GOD's grace will eventually be won.

Peace and Blessings. To GOD be the Glory!